Bug detective

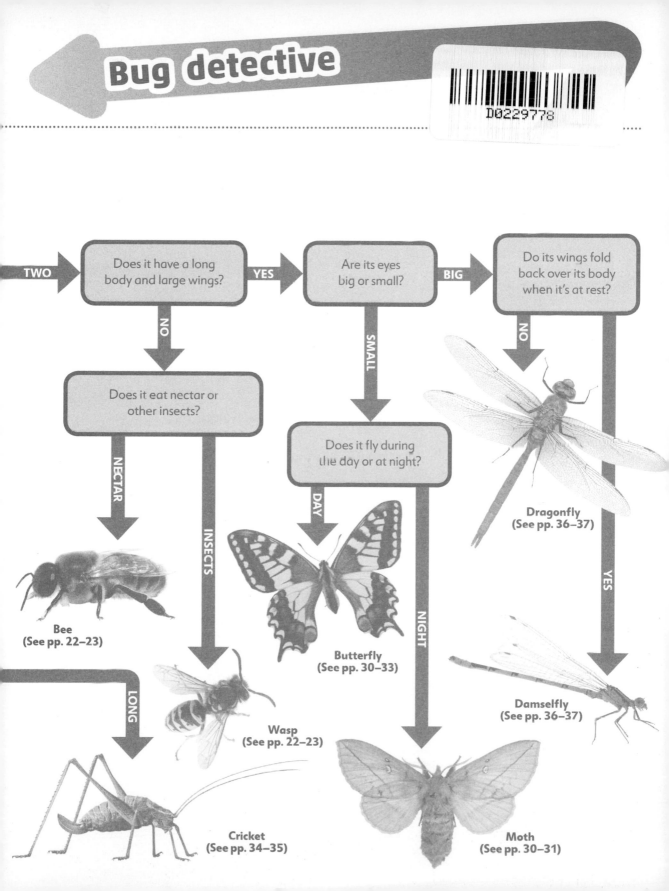

TWO → Does it have a long body and large wings? → **YES** → Are its eyes big or small? → **BIG** → Do its wings fold back over its body when it's at rest?

Does it have a long body and large wings? → **NO** → Does it eat nectar or other insects?

Does it eat nectar or other insects? → **NECTAR** → **Bee** (See pp. 22–23)

Does it eat nectar or other insects? → **INSECTS** → **Wasp** (See pp. 22–23)

LONG → **Cricket** (See pp. 34–35)

Are its eyes big or small? → **SMALL** → Does it fly during the day or at night?

Does it fly during the day or at night? → **DAY** → **Butterfly** (See pp. 30–33)

Does it fly during the day or at night? → **NIGHT** → **Moth** (See pp. 30–31)

Do its wings fold back over its body when it's at rest? → **NO** → **Dragonfly** (See pp. 36–37)

Do its wings fold back over its body when it's at rest? → **YES** → **Damselfly** (See pp. 36–37)

Things to find out:

DK findout!

Bugs

Author: Andrea Mills
Subject consultant: Kristie Reddick

DK | Penguin Random House

Project editors Allison Singer, Satu Fox, Ishani Nandi
Senior art editor Katie Knutton
Project art editor Joanne Clark
Editorial assistant Megan Weal
Additional design Bettina Myklebust Stovne
Art editors Nehal Verma, Kartik Gera
Assistant art editor Jaileen Kaur
Managing editors Laura Gilbert, Alka Thakur Hazarika
Managing art editors Diane Peyton Jones, Romi Chakraborty
Pre-production producer Dragana Puvacic
Producer Srijana Gurung
Art director Martin Wilson
Publisher Sarah Larter
Publishing director Sophie Mitchell

Educational consultant Jacqueline Harris

First published in Great Britain in 2017 by
Dorling Kindersley Limited
80 Strand, London, WC2R 0RL

A CIP catalogue record for this book
is available from the British Library.
ISBN: 978-0-2412-8473-5

Printed and bound in China

A WORLD OF IDEAS:
SEE ALL THERE IS TO KNOW

www.dk.com

The scale boxes in this book show how big a bug is compared to a person's hand – about 203 mm (7 in) long – or thumb – around 68 mm (2⅝ in) long.

» Scale

» Scale

Contents

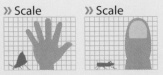

Goliath beetle

Common field grasshopper

Seven-spot ladybird

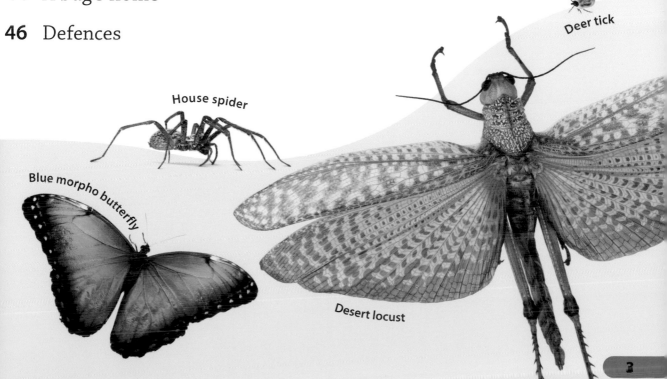

House spider

Blue morpho butterfly

Desert locust

Deer tick

How it began

The story of bugs begins with the story of arthropods. Arthropods are the most successful animal group of all time. They have hard outer skeletons, legs with joints, and segmented bodies. The first arthropods developed on Earth more than 500 million years ago (MYA).

540 MYA
Early arthropods – worm-like creatures with thick skin like an outer skeleton – move along on the sea floor.

Ancient griffenflies looked a lot like this dragonfly, but much bigger.

320 MYA
Over time, insects on land develop wings and are the first animals to fly – and the only flying animals for 100 million years.

350 MYA
Land arthropods grow in size, too – like this huge millipede, which could have been 2 m (7 ft) long!

Griffenfly
This early insect had a long body and a wingspan of up to 75 cm (30 in).

270 MYA
Dinosaurs first appear on Earth. Some dinosaurs and other animals hunt and eat the bigger arthropods.

How do we know?

Fossils are the remains of creatures preserved for many millions of years. They give us a clear look at the arthropods of the past.

Spider in amber
This ancient spider got caught in sticky tree sap, which hardened into a fossil. It shows that spiders have looked the same since they first appeared nearly 420 MYA.

438–408 MYA
Most arthropods are small. Some, like this sea scorpion, grow big and are the first predators, or animals that attack and eat other animals.

Trilobite
Tiny trilobites were common on the sea floor. They had two feelers (antennae) and a body split in three sections, like modern-day insects.

428 MYA
Millipedes come out of the ocean and become the first-ever animals to walk on land.

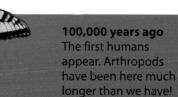

230–73 MYA
Many arthropods we see today, such as insects and other bugs, begin to appear.

100,000 years ago
The first humans appear. Arthropods have been here much longer than we have!

Trilobite fossil
Preserved in rock, this trilobite fossil is one of many found on the sea floor. Trilobites don't exist today, so fossils are our only way of knowing what these very early arthropods looked like.

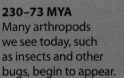

! WOW!
Today, about **80 per cent** of all known **animals** are **arthropods.**

North America

This continent has grasslands, forests, mountains, and deserts – and all kinds of bugs to match! One of these is the monarch butterfly. Groups of monarchs travel 5,000 km (3,100 miles) from Canada to Mexico every year. This is called migration.

South America

The Earth's largest rainforest is the Amazon. It stretches across nine countries in South America and is home to more than 2.5 million species of insect. This continent has many leaf-carrying ants and mound-building termites.

Migrating monarchs

Monarch butterfly

Leafcutter ant carrying part of a leaf

Leafcutter ant

Termite

Termite mound in Brazil

A world of bugs

Bugs live all over the world. They can be found on every continent and in every climate. These creatures are the ultimate survivors, making themselves at home in sizzling hot deserts, on snowy mountaintops, and everywhere in between.

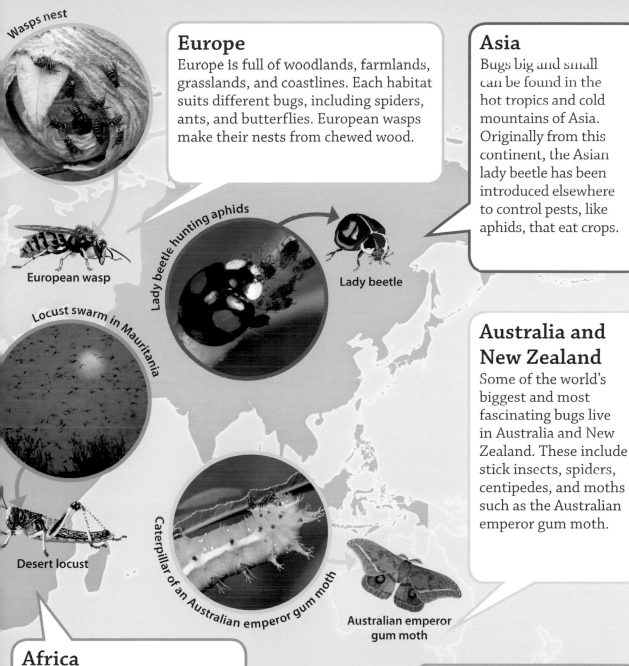

Wasps nest

Europe

Europe is full of woodlands, farmlands, grasslands, and coastlines. Each habitat suits different bugs, including spiders, ants, and butterflies. European wasps make their nests from chewed wood.

Asia

Bugs big and small can be found in the hot tropics and cold mountains of Asia. Originally from this continent, the Asian lady beetle has been introduced elsewhere to control pests, like aphids, that eat crops.

European wasp

Lady beetle hunting aphids

Lady beetle

Locust swarm in Mauritania

Australia and New Zealand

Some of the world's biggest and most fascinating bugs live in Australia and New Zealand. These include stick insects, spiders, centipedes, and moths such as the Australian emperor gum moth.

Desert locust

Caterpillar of an Australian emperor gum moth

Australian emperor gum moth

Africa

Africa is the hottest continent. More than half its land is dry or desert. Bugs must survive in high temperatures and with little food or water. Here, locusts swarm in the skies looking for crops to eat.

Antarctica

The icy ground and freezing temperatures of Antarctica are too much for most bugs. Only the chironomid midge has what it takes to live here year-round.

Chironomid midge

Senses

Bugs have super senses to help them survive. They share the same senses as humans – sight, smell, touch, taste, and hearing. These are used to find food, escape from predators, and meet mates. Like humans, bugs can sense hot or cold and whether something is wet or dry. They also know if they are the right way up or upside down.

HEARING

GRASSHOPPER

Although bugs don't have ears, they are sensitive to sound. Many sense sound vibrations in the air through their skin. Some have a tympanal organ, which is a special feature on their bodies that helps them to hear. Grasshoppers have their tympanal organ on their stomach.

SMELL

FIG WASP

Instead of noses, bugs use their sensitive antennae to pick up scents. These long feelers are covered in nerve endings that sense chemical changes in the air. Wasps, like the fig wasp, are super smellers. Some scientists think they can smell as well as dogs can!

TOUCH

JEWEL BEETLE

Bugs use their antennae to feel their surroundings. Some bugs also have sensitive hairs on their abdomen (stomach) that can pick up on moving air, allowing them to sense if there are any predators or prey nearby.

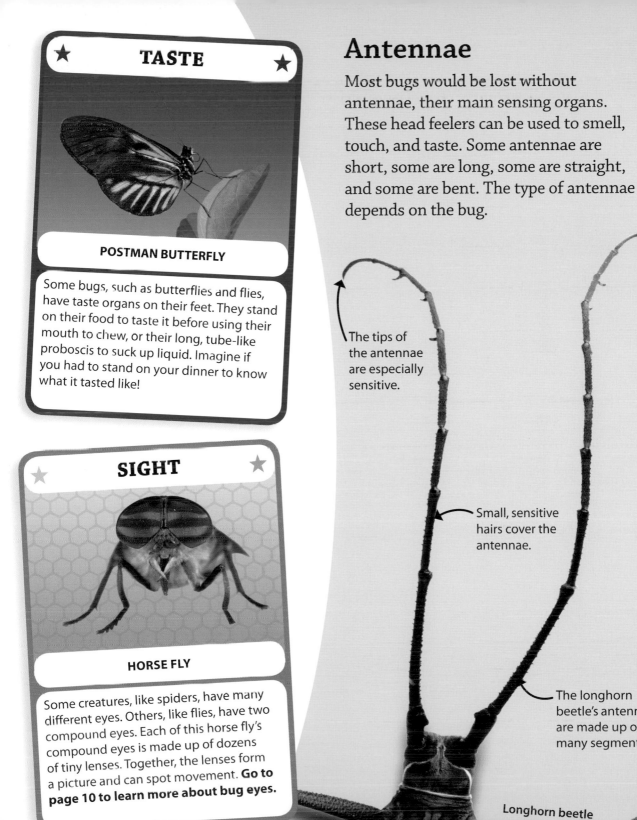

TASTE

POSTMAN BUTTERFLY

Some bugs, such as butterflies and flies, have taste organs on their feet. They stand on their food to taste it before using their mouth to chew, or their long, tube-like proboscis to suck up liquid. Imagine if you had to stand on your dinner to know what it tasted like!

SIGHT

HORSE FLY

Some creatures, like spiders, have many different eyes. Others, like flies, have two compound eyes. Each of this horse fly's compound eyes is made up of dozens of tiny lenses. Together, the lenses form a picture and can spot movement. **Go to page 10 to learn more about bug eyes.**

Antennae

Most bugs would be lost without antennae, their main sensing organs. These head feelers can be used to smell, touch, and taste. Some antennae are short, some are long, some are straight, and some are bent. The type of antennae depends on the bug.

The tips of the antennae are especially sensitive.

Small, sensitive hairs cover the antennae.

The longhorn beetle's antennae are made up of many segments.

Longhorn beetle

Eye spy

Bugs see the world very differently to us. Most have at least two eyes and can have two types of vision. Simple eyes are small and can sense light and dark. Compound eyes, like those of a dragonfly, are larger. They are made up of lots of tiny lenses and give a different kind of sight. Some lucky bugs, such as the grasshopper, have both kinds of eyes.

! REALLY?

A dragonfly can have up to **30,000 lenses** in each eyeball.

Extreme eyes

Some eyes must be seen to be believed. These bugs use their unusual-looking eyes to their advantage.

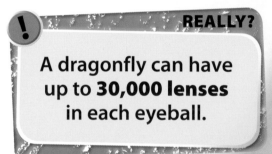

Each eyestalk is about 0.5 cm (¼ in) long.

Out of sight
The Malaysian stalk-eyed fly's eyes stand out on stalks. This helps them to see more of the world around them.

Compound eyes

Compound eyes have lots of tiny lenses, giving the bug a mosaic, or pieced-together, view. Bugs with big compound eyes can see in nearly all directions. Compound eyes are also excellent at sensing movement, which helps the bug hunt for food or avoid attackers.

Dragonfly
With eyes covering most of their head, dragonflies have incredible eyesight. They see more colours and detail than most other bugs.

This looks like an eye, but it's a fake!

Side eyes are used to detect motion.

Eye to eye
Tropical jumping spiders have eight eyes – two at the front that see colours and see in focus, and three more on each side.

Great pretender
The swallowtail caterpillar has a clever method of self-defence. The patterns on its skin look like eyes, but its real eyes are hidden under its body.

Time to eat

Just like all other living creatures, bugs need to eat in order to survive. Some bugs eat plants or plant matter, while others prefer meat and other animal matter. There are bugs that enjoy a mixed menu of both meat and plants. Blood and nectar are popular with some bugs, too.

Plant-eaters

Plants are in good supply in most areas, so they are a major food source. Bugs munch through their wood, leaves, roots, and seeds. Even algae, an underwater plant, can be a tasty snack for bugs that live near ponds.

Pollen from the flower sticks to the bee's fur.

When plants bite back

Some surprising plants turn nature on its head by eating meat. The Venus fly trap is one of these meat-eaters. It has moving parts that help it to catch insects and spiders.

Prey, such as this damselfly, walks onto or lands on the sensitive bristles of the open Venus fly trap.

The trap snaps shut so the prey can't escape. Now it can begin to digest, or break down, its catch.

Meat-eaters

Hunting is hard work. Many winged bugs fly about looking for prey. Others lie in wait for prey to pass instead. Scavenger bugs feed on other hunters' leftovers. Some true flies, like female mosquitoes, drink the blood of live animals.

Aphids are also known as plant lice or greenflies.

Tasty leaves
Leaves are a common food source for many bugs, like caterpillars. They chew their way through crunchy green leaves, such as those from this cherry tree.

Sweet drink
Bees drink a sugary fluid called nectar, found inside flowering plants. They use the nectar to make honey back at the hive.

Wasp hunter
The assassin bug grabs its prey, stabs the body with its sharp proboscis, and fills the wasp with toxic saliva. The saliva turns the wasp's insides to liquid, which the assassin bug can then drink.

Picking off pests
Ladybirds have an appetite for aphids, which are small, sap-sucking pests. Aphids pose a threat to plants, so ladybirds are a helpful form of pest control.

On the move

Whether scuttling, swimming, or soaring, bugs have different ways of getting around. Most use their legs to move on land, but some take to the skies or make a splash underwater.

Caterpillars climb up plants and feed on their leaves.

Death's head hawk-moth caterpillar

Climbing

Having lots of legs comes in handy when climbing steep tree trunks and plant stems. Some bugs have claws to hold on tight, or sticky feet to give grip.

Lacewings usually come out to fly and feed after dark.

Lacewing

Flying

Insects were the first creatures to fly, 150 million years before birds did. Insects like this lacewing are expert fliers thanks to their two sets of fast-flapping wings.

Scuttling

Some bugs, including carpenter ants, spend their lives on land. They use their lightweight bodies and multiple legs to scuttle around at high speed.

Carpenter ant

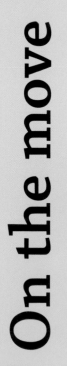

WOW!

One per cent of the total number of insects in the world are ants.

Walking on water

The tiny bits of water at the surface of a pond stick together, forming something called surface tension. Special insects and spiders with long legs and waterproof feet are able to scurry across it.

Pond skaters move across the water at 1.5 m (5 ft) per second.

Pond skater from above

Pond skater

Swimming

The young of some bugs live in water, often moving along the pond or lake bed. Some adult bugs are powerful swimmers, using their legs as oars.

Sunburst diving beetle

This beetle carries an air bubble so it can breathe underwater.

Legs

Most bugs need their legs to get around or hunt for food. The three most common kinds of bug legs are running, jumping, and grasping.

Running
Cockroaches can run at high speeds thanks to their strong, quick-moving legs.

Jumping
Grasshoppers push off their powerful back legs when they jump.

Grasping
The praying mantis uses its spiky front legs like hands when hunting for its next meal.

What is an insect?

The arthropod group includes all sorts of amazing bugs, from the creepy-crawlies that scuttle and squirm across the ground to the winged wonders that fly through our gardens. By far the biggest group of arthropods is insects. All insects have six legs and three-part bodies. They come in many shapes and sizes, and have features that make them easy to spot.

Antenna

Many insects, like the red giraffe weevil, have two long feelers (antennae) coming out of their head. These antennae help them to touch, taste, hear, and smell what's around them.

Red giraffe weevil

Eyes

Some insects, such as this dragonfly, have eyes with lots of tiny lenses. These are called compound eyes. They let them see in almost every direction.

Dragonfly

Mouthparts

Some insects have powerful jaws to catch and chew food. Others, including the swallowtail butterfly, have a straw-like tube called a proboscis for sucking food.

Swallowtail butterfly

Praying mantis

Wings

Most flying insects, like this giant atlas moth, have two pairs of wings. True flies are the only insects that have one pair. Insect wings are often see-through and thin, but tough.

Giant atlas moth

Elytra

Many insects, such as the golden beetle, have hard wings called elytra that look like a shell. Elytra hide a second, softer set of wings underneath.

Golden beetle

Body

All insect bodies, like this ant's, are divided into three parts – head, thorax (chest), and abdomen (stomach).

Winged black garden ant

Stinger

European wasp

Bees, wasps, and hornets have stingers that release venom when injected into skin. Wasps and hornets can sting repeatedly.

Legs

All insects have three pairs of legs attached to their thorax (chest). The praying mantis uses its big front legs to seize prey in a split second.

Incredible insects

There are more insects than any other creatures in the world. At least one million types have been named so far, and more are being named all the time. Insects are divided into groups based on their features. Here are a few of the major groups you'll meet in this book.

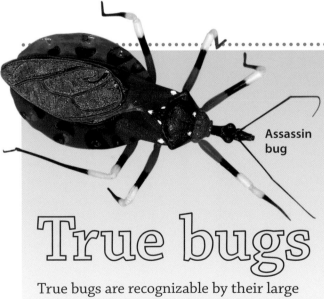

Assassin bug

True bugs

True bugs are recognizable by their large antennae, their soft bodies, and the sharp mouthparts that pierce their food. One bloodthirsty true bug is the assassin bug, which sucks the blood of birds and reptiles.

Ants, bees, and wasps

Ants build nests where they live in huge numbers. Bees and wasps are bigger, buzzing insects with stingers. Many people don't realize that ants are in the same group as bees and wasps, but their segmented bodies are quite similar.

Wasp

True flies

Most insects have four wings, but true flies have only two. Instead of a second pair of wings, they have knob-like features called halteres that help them to fly. There are more than 100,000 kinds of true fly.

Green bottle fly

Golden beetle

BEETLES

There are more than 400,000 types of beetle. Their shiny bodies make them easy to spot. This golden beetle's hard covering looks like a shell, but it's really one of the beetle's two sets of wings.

Grasshoppers and crickets

This is a noisy group of insects! Grasshoppers sing by rubbing their legs over their wings, and crickets chirp by rubbing their wings together. Both of these creatures have biting mouths and long legs for jumping.

Painted grasshopper

Dragonfly

Dragonflies and damselflies

Dragonflies and damselflies are skilled hunters. They use their excellent eyesight to target and catch other insects to eat. These high-speed fliers look graceful as they zoom through the air.

Jewel beetles

At home in tropical regions, these dazzling beetles stand out due to the brilliant colours of their elytra.

Jewel weevil

Jewel beetle

Stag beetles

The male stag beetle has big pincer-like jaws for attracting females and battling other males. They can fight, but sometimes they just open up their elytra, flap their wings, and fly off.

Stag beetle

Leaf beetles

As their name suggests, leaf beetles feed on most vegetation, including plants and flowers. They come in different sizes, shapes, colours, and patterns.

Lily leaf beetle

Beetles

Beetles are the biggest insect group. They make up nearly half of all insect species on Earth. You can recognize a beetle by its shiny outer wings, called elytra, which look like a shell and cover a second, softer set of wings. About 400,000 species have been named so far, and experts think there may be at least four million species in total.

Longhorn beetles

With eye-catching patterns and huge jaws, longhorn beetles are a spectacular sight, especially when they fly. Their antennae can grow as long as their body – or, for some, even longer!

Longhorn beetle

Being a beetle

Like all other bugs, beetles need certain things in order to survive. They need to lay eggs so more beetles will hatch into the world, they need to eat food so they can grow and have energy, and they need to find a safe place to live.

ACTUAL SIZE!

Goliath beetle

Scarab beetles

Scarabs, like this goliath beetle, are a group of beetle found in most parts of the world. They are known for their antennae, the ends of which can open and close like little fans.

Ladybirds

Ladybirds

These beetles have bright colours and large spots meant to scare off predators. They can also release an unpleasant scent to make themselves seem like an unappealing meal.

Colorado beetle tending to its eggs

Laying eggs
Female beetles can lay hundreds of tiny eggs in one go on leaves or wood. The eggs will begin hatching after a few days or weeks, releasing the new beetles (larvae).

Blister beetle eating a leaf

Eating
Many beetles eat plant matter, such as leaves, fruit, and seeds. Some hunt small creatures, while others munch on fungus or dung.

Diving beetle going for a swim

Habitats
Beetles are found in nearly every habitat, from forests and deserts to rivers and lakes. They can live anywhere there is plenty of food for them to eat.

Bees and wasps

Bees and wasps both have six legs, three-part bodies, and two pairs of see-through wings. To be able to tell these two buzzing insects apart, you'll need a closer look.

Hair Grains of pollen get caught in hair all over a bee's body.

Antennae Two bent feelers pick up smells.

Legs Bees can collect pollen in the hollow, flat part of their hind legs.

Abdomen Bees drink nectar, and their abdomen can hold lots of it.

Mouthparts Bees have jaws for chewing and a long, sticky tongue for sucking up nectar.

Ants

Like bees, ants have bent feelers, which can be used to feed their young. Bees, wasps, and ants all build very organised homes and work hard to maintain them.

Extra-long feelers The feelers, or antennae, contain the touch and smell organs. Ants use touch to greet each other and smell to find their way home.

Wasps

Wasps have slim, smooth bodies. They hunt insects as prey. Some wasps live in nests with others, but many wasps prefer to live and hunt alone.

Common wasp

» **Length:** 1.5 cm (⅝ in)

» **Diet:** Insects

» **Lifespan:** Up to three weeks

Stingers
Wasp stingers are smooth. Only female wasps and bees have stingers.

Hair Wasps have some hair, but they are much smoother than bees.

Body A wasp's body is lean and perfect for flying fast and hunting.

Antennae Wasps have two feelers without joints.

Mouthparts Wasps have large, biting jaws to chew and tear their food.

Legs All of a wasp's legs are cylindrical, not flat.

Super strong
Ants have super strength. An ant can carry up to 50 times its own body weight.

Army of ants
Ants live in large colonies ruled by a queen. Worker ants build the nest, search for food, and protect the young.

True bugs

People use the word "bug" to describe all sorts of creepy-crawlies. But, actually, true bugs are a special type of insect with a long, pokey mouthpart called a rostrum. They use their rostrum to pierce and drink their food.

Colours
True bugs come in many colours. Some are dark or spotted, which helps with camouflage. Others are brightly coloured, which helps scare off attackers.

Wings
True bugs are in the Hemiptera group, which means "half-wing" in Greek. Some have forewings that are partly see-through, so they look like half a wing.

Jointed legs
Like all insects, true bugs have six legs split into three pairs. Each leg has jointed sections, which helps with walking and, for certain true bugs, springing.

Closer look

What separates true bugs most from other insects are their special wings and piercing mouthparts. Let's take a closer look at both of these features in action.

Mouthparts
True bugs are mostly known for their long, beak-like rostrum, which both looks and works like a sharp straw.

Winging it
True bugs, like this stink bug, have special forewings. The front part of the forewing is hard, while the back part is softer and more see-through.

Hard part of forewing

Softer, more see-through part of forewing

See-through hind wing used to flap and fly

Wheel bug

Stick and suck
True bugs use their sharp rostrum to pierce food and suck it up. Some drink sap from plants, while others are predators, which means they hunt other insects or drink animal blood.

! WOW!

This **jewel bug** can release a **super strong stink** if it feels threatened.

Water scorpion bug piercing and eating a damselfly nymph

25

True flies

Most insects in this group have just one pair of wings. Instead of the second pair found on other flying insects, true flies have tiny, shrivelled, club-shaped organs called halteres. Halteres help true flies balance while they fly.

! WOW!

True flies eat **everything** from **blood** to **rubbish**. They're not **picky!**

House fly

These flies are found in most places humans are. They are scavengers, which means they look for dead or rotting food to eat.

A house fly's wings can beat 200 times a second.

Haltere

FACT FILE

» **Length:** 12 mm (1/2 in)

» **Diet:** Rotten food and rubbish

» **Habitat:** Farmland, houses, and gardens

» Scale

FACT FILE

» **Length:** 15 mm (5/8 in)

» **Diet:** Nectar from flowers

» **Habitat:** Gardens and fields

» Scale

Like all true flies, drone flies don't have a stinger.

Drone fly

The drone fly is a type of European hover fly. Its black and orange or yellow stripes make it look like a honeybee.

Bat fly

Bat flies are unusual creatures with no eyes or wings. They are parasites, living in bats' fur and feeding off their blood.

» Scale

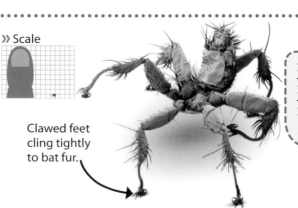

Clawed feet cling tightly to bat fur.

FACT FILE

» **Length:** 2 mm (1/10 in)

» **Diet:** Blood

» **Habitat:** Bat fur

A pair of tiny sponges called labella soak up liquids like nectar.

FACT FILE

» **Length:** Up to 60 mm (2 ³/₀ in)

» **Diet:** Nectar from flowers

» **Habitat:** Hot regions with plants and bushes

Wingspan up to 50 mm (2 in) long

Mydas fly

Some of the largest true flies are mydas flies, like this species from South America. Despite its intimidating size, it is harmless.

Long, slim abdomen

» Scale

Mosquito

Most people don't think of a mosquito as a fly, but that's exactly what it is! Like all true flies, mosquitoes have one pair of wings. Male mosquitoes sip nectar, while female mosquitoes prefer blood.

FACT FILE

» **Length:** Up to 25 mm (1 in)

» **Diet:** Nectar and pollen

» **Habitat:** Sandy, rocky areas

» Scale

Bee fly

With their fat, furry bodies, bee flies look like bumblebees. They lay eggs on other insects so their larvae can feed on insect blood until they grow up.

Extra long proboscis

Robber fly

Unlike most true flies, the robber fly attacks other insects. It injects deadly venom into its prey's body before sucking up the soft insides.

» Scale

Large eyes for hunting prey

FACT FILE

» **Length:** Up to 50 mm (2 in)

» **Diet:** Other insects

» **Habitat:** Hot, dry areas

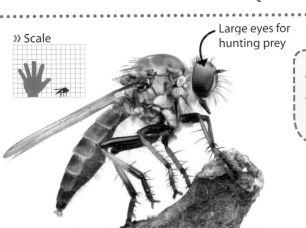

Dragonflies

Two sets of wings that can be flapped separately help dragonflies to reach speeds of 50 kph (30 mph).

True flies

Flies can fly forwards, backwards, sideways, or hover in the air. Tiny knobs behind the wings, called halteres, help flies to sense if they are off balance.

Hover fly

Southern hawker dragonfly

Beetles

The delicate wings of beetles such as ladybirds are protected by two hard outer wings called elytra.

Seven-spot ladybird

Veins make wings stronger.

Wings

Many insects take to the air to find food, hunt prey, escape predators, or meet a mate. Most have two sets of wings, but some, such as true flies, have only one set. Insect wings are usually very thin, with veins running through them that make them strong.

Grasshoppers and locusts

Most grasshoppers and locusts have two pairs of wings. One set is narrow and strong, while the other is wide and bendy.

True bugs

The wings of a true bug lay flat over their backs and form a cross when they aren't flying. The shield bug is known for its noisy, buzzing flight.

Shield bug

Butterflies and moths

Butterfly and moth wings are some of the most detailed. Their wings are covered in tiny overlapping scales. The scales are made of similar material to your fingernails.

Swallowtail butterfly

The microscopic scales form patterns.

Desert locust

WOW!

Some grasshopper wings are **ten times thinner** than a **human hair.**

Bees and wasps

These buzzing insects have two pairs of see-through wings. Bees and wasps have a row of hooks that can stick the pairs of wings together to beat at the same time.

Common wasp

Butterflies

Butterflies are colourful insects with patterned wings. Like many insects, they have six jointed legs, eyes with lots of lenses, and long antennae. These fantastic fliers can be found in most parts of the world.

Blue morpho butterfly

This butterfly's striking blue wings make it easy to spot.

Butterflies rest with their wings closed and upright.

Cardinal butterfly

Cairns birdwing butterfly

These long antennae can touch, smell, and sense vibrations.

Can you guess?

It can be tricky to tell a moth from a butterfly. Can you guess which insect each of these features belongs to? Use the pictures to help you.

1

This insect's soft colours help it to blend in with its environment.

2

This insect has short, feathery antennae that have more than 30,000 sensors.

...and moths

Moths are closely related to butterflies. Some moths are colourful, while others have darker colours and simple patterns to help them blend in with leafy woodlands. Most rest during the day before coming out to fly at night.

Silk moth

A moth's antennae are shorter than a butterfly's.

Moths rest with their wings open and flat.

Drinker moth

Sandy carpet moth

Many moths have hairy bodies.

3

This insect has long antennae and a proboscis that is curled up until it's time to eat.

4

A hairy body may help this insect to stay warm when it flies at night.

5

The bright colours of this insect can be seen in the daytime when it flies.

Becoming a butterfly

Butterflies are one of the many incredible insects that totally change their appearance in the natural world's most amazing process. This process is called metamorphosis.

Antennae help the butterfly to smell nectar and keep its balance.

The butterfly will start flying within hours of leaving its chrysalis.

Stages of life

A butterfly egg goes through many changes before a new butterfly can take flight. The entire process can take between a month and a year, depending on the species.

1 Egg
Butterfly eggs are laid on plants. The butterfly type determines the eggs' size, shape, and colour.

2 Caterpillar
Tiny caterpillars hatch from the eggs. They are very hungry and start eating leaves right away. They grow quickly.

3 Chrysalis
Once grown, the caterpillar wraps itself in a chrysalis and re-forms as a butterfly. Inside this chrysalis is a butterfly nearly ready to break out.

4 Adult

The chrysalis splits, revealing a butterfly ready to spread its new wings. This North American monarch butterfly will feed on sweet nectar from flowers to gain the energy it needs to fly.

Laying eggs

Adult female butterflies look for a mate, then lay their eggs on a plant. The eggs will soon hatch, and the metamorphosis cycle will begin all over again.

Crickets and grasshoppers

These noisy insects "sing" by rubbing parts of their bodies together to attract a mate. Locusts, a kind of grasshopper, and katydids, a kind of cricket, have extra-long legs that help them to hop.

Common field grasshopper

This grasshopper is known for its hairy chest! It can fly fast, and sometimes many of them swarm together.

Grasshoppers make noise by rubbing their hind legs against their wings.

FACT FILE

» **Length:** Up to 25 mm (1 in)
» **Diet:** Mainly plants
» **Habitat:** Fields and grasslands

» Scale

FACT FILE

» **Length:** Up to 20 mm (¾ in)
» **Diet:** Insects and vegetation
» **Habitat:** Grasslands

» Scale

» Scale

Bush cricket

Bush crickets come in lots of colours. They can't fly, so they use their powerful back legs to jump.

FACT FILE

» **Length:** Up to 50 mm (2 in)
» **Diet:** Vegetation and insects
» **Habitat:** African bush

Armoured ground cricket

These flightless African insects look incredible in their sturdy body armour. Their thorax is covered in spines for extra defence.

Leaf-mimic katydid

The leaf-mimic katydid does an amazing impression of a dead leaf to avoid being eaten. It listens using hearing organs on its legs.

Its body looks veined and dry, like a dead leaf.

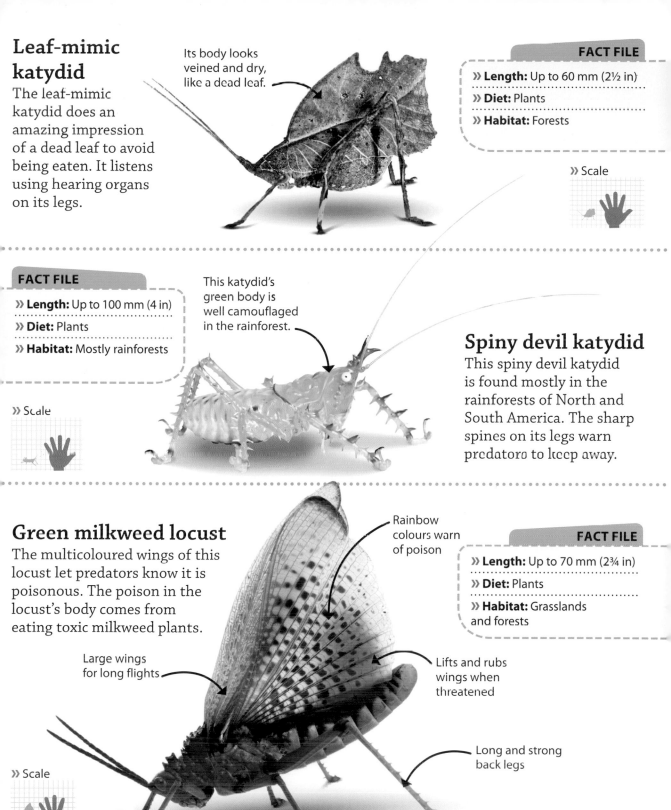

This katydid's green body is well camouflaged in the rainforest.

Spiny devil katydid

This spiny devil katydid is found mostly in the rainforests of North and South America. The sharp spines on its legs warn predators to keep away.

Green milkweed locust

The multicoloured wings of this locust let predators know it is poisonous. The poison in the locust's body comes from eating toxic milkweed plants.

Rainbow colours warn of poison

Large wings for long flights

Lifts and rubs wings when threatened

Long and strong back legs

Dragonflies and damselflies

Darting across ponds and rivers, dragonflies and damselflies are speedy hunters looking for insects to eat. They all have big compound eyes and two pairs of wings. Dragonflies are usually larger, stronger, and faster than damselflies.

Common darter

Named for its hunting style, this dragonfly darts off a perch to catch an insect in flight. Then it flies back to the same perch to eat it.

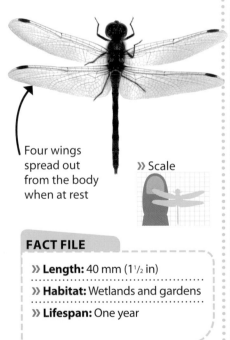

Four wings spread out from the body when at rest

» Scale

FACT FILE

» **Length:** 40 mm (1½ in)

» **Habitat:** Wetlands and gardens

» **Lifespan:** One year

Crimson marsh glider

This colourful dragonfly shines in direct sunlight, but it can hide among flowers.

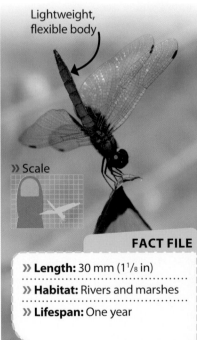

Lightweight, flexible body

» Scale

FACT FILE

» **Length:** 30 mm (1⅛ in)

» **Habitat:** Rivers and marshes

» **Lifespan:** One year

Broad-bodied chaser

As its name gives away, the broad-bodied chaser has both a wide middle and an appetite for chasing other insects.

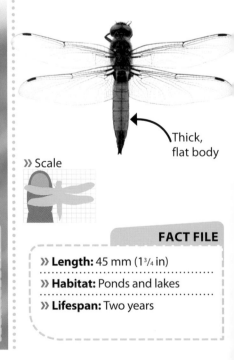

Thick, flat body

» Scale

FACT FILE

» **Length:** 45 mm (1¾ in)

» **Habitat:** Ponds and lakes

» **Lifespan:** Two years

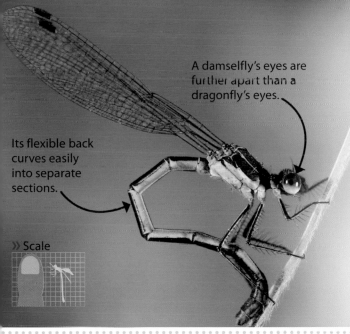

A damselfly's eyes are further apart than a dragonfly's eyes.

Its flexible back curves easily into separate sections.

» Scale

Scarce emerald damselfly

A striking emerald-green colour, this damselfly blends in with waterside reeds for safety from any attackers, such as birds and small lizards.

FACT FILE

» **Length:** 35 mm (1¼ in)

» **Habitat:** Thick plant areas and near shallow waters

» **Lifespan:** Six months

Small red damselfly

This small, stunning damselfly is a fragile, weak flier. As a result, it stays close to water and does not travel far.

FACT FILE

» **Length:** 30 mm (1⅛ in)

» **Habitat:** Ponds and streams

» **Lifespan:** Six months

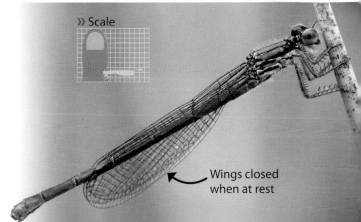

» Scale

Wings closed when at rest

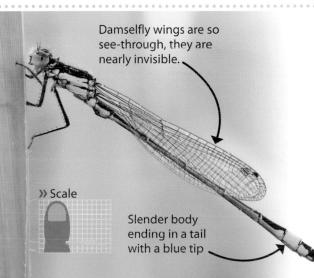

Damselfly wings are so see-through, they are nearly invisible.

» Scale

Slender body ending in a tail with a blue tip

Blue-tailed damselfly

This damselfly has a partially blue body, blue tail, and blue eyes. It is known to eat insects that have become caught in spider webs.

FACT FILE

» **Length:** 30 mm (1⅛ in)

» **Habitat:** Lakes, ponds, and heathlands

» **Lifespan:** Six months

Insect relatives

Insects aren't the only amazing animals in the arthropod group. All arthropods, from eight-legged arachnids to many-legged myriapods, are related by their jointed legs, segmented bodies, and a hard outer shell. They are also invertebrates, which are animals without a backbone.

Stinger filled with venom

Emperor scorpion

Scorpions

Scorpions are arachnids with body armour. They either crush their prey with their strong pincers or inject venom into it from the stinger at the end of their tail.

Velvet mites

Mites and ticks

These tiny arachnids are parasites. That means they live on other living creatures and feed on their blood for survival.

Deer ticks

Giant desert hairy scorpion

Imperial scorpion

Centipedes can regrow their legs if they come off.

Giant tiger centipede

Myriapods

Myriapods, such as millipedes and centipedes, are arthropods with lots of legs. Centipedes have one pair of legs on each body segment, while millipedes have two pairs on each segment.

Giant millipede

Harvestmen

These arachnids look like skinny spiders. However, they have only two eyes, not eight, and they don't have any venom.

Armoured millipede

Harvestmen can lose their legs to escape danger.

Burmese millipede

House spider

Spiders

About half of all arachnids are spiders. They usually have eight eyes and eight legs. Most have sharp fangs they use to inject venom into their prey.

Desert blonde tarantula

ACTUAL SIZE!

The tarantula's hairy legs can sense movement from nearby prey, such as beetles, and predators, such as snakes.

Gooty tarantula

Cave spider

Spider crabs use their sensitive legs to find food.

Spiny spider crab

Crustaceans

They may not look like other bugs, but crustaceans such as crabs and lobsters are also arthropods. They are even sometimes called the "bugs of the sea".

Hermit crab

American lobster

Horseshoe crab

This unusual arthropod isn't a crab, or even a crustacean. It is part of a family of arthropods known as Merostomata. Called "living fossils", horseshoe crabs look almost exactly the same as they did 300 million years ago.

The horseshoe crab's tail helps it to swim. Its spikes are for protection.

Meet the experts

Meet bug experts Kristie Reddick and Jessica Honaker. Kristie and Jessica are entomologists, or scientists who study bugs. Together, they run an entomology website, make amazing videos, and travel all over the world as The Bug Chicks.

Q: We know it is something to do with bugs, but what do you actually do?

A: When we were at university, Jessica studied aphids that eat farmers' crops, and how to reduce how many chemicals (pesticides) farmers use. Kristie studied solifuge arachnids, which are cousins of spiders, in Africa. She discovered a new species and observed what these animals eat and what eats them. Now we teach about the amazing world of insects, spiders, and their relatives.

Kristie studied this species of solifuge arachnid in Kenya. In this picture it is munching on a grasshopper.

Q: What made you both decide that you wanted to be entomologists?

A: Bugs are so cool! From pests to pollinators, they are everywhere on the planet, and our world wouldn't be the same without them. Bugs are endlessly fascinating, so we will never be bored!

Q: Is there special equipment you use when working with bugs?

A: Entomologists use lots of different tools to collect and study bugs. We use nets to sweep grasses and the air, aspirators to suck up tiny bugs from plants, and pitfall traps to catch bugs on the ground. We also use a technique called "night lighting" – we hang up a white sheet at night and shine lights on it to attract nocturnal insects. We have an "arthropod zoo" in our office, so we use lots of cages to keep them safe.

Q: What is a usual work day for you?

A: As The Bug Chicks, we spend a lot of time teaching young people about bugs. We travel to schools and libraries to speak and show our arthropod zoo. We also make videos and write on our blog.

Kristie checks elephant dung for signs of bugs.

The Bug Chicks' arthropod zoo is filmed.

Q: What is the best part of your job?

A: We love changing people's minds about insects and spiders. It's incredible helping people conquer their fears.

Q: What do you wish more people knew about bugs?

A: That they are not out to get us! Without bugs the world wouldn't work how it needs to for us to survive. Bugs are recyclers and pollinators and food sources for lots of other animals. Let's show them respect!

Q: What are the biggest problems facing bugs today?

A: The loss of their habitats, and farmers who use too many or the wrong kinds of pesticides. There are so many new species of bug that we are losing as our forests disappear and people build on land where bugs used to live. Also, many helpful insects like honeybees are struggling due to the chemicals farmers use.

Q: What can we do to help bugs?

A: People could help bugs by not spraying or killing every bug they see right away. If you find an insect or a spider in your home, consider carefully putting it outside and letting it go instead. Don't just spray it with chemicals or step on it. Bugs are animals, and they deserve to be here, too.

Jessica holds a friendly millipede.

Bug watch

Heading off on a bug hunt is lots of fun, and you never know what you'll find in the great outdoors. Be patient, keep your eyes peeled, and handle bugs with care and consideration. Here are some top tips for budding bug hunters.

Do research

Find out all you can about the bugs you are interested in by looking them up in books or on helpful websites.

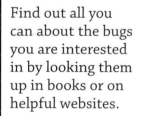

Get your tools

Gather a net and a tray or jar to collect bugs in. (But don't leave a jar's lid on tightly – bugs need air to breathe.)

Find a spot

Go to the countryside, a wooded area, or a nearby park. You can find bugs by trees, under rocks, and in the grass.

Hunt for signs

Look all around for evidence of bug activity, such as chewed leaves or carefully crafted nests and webs.

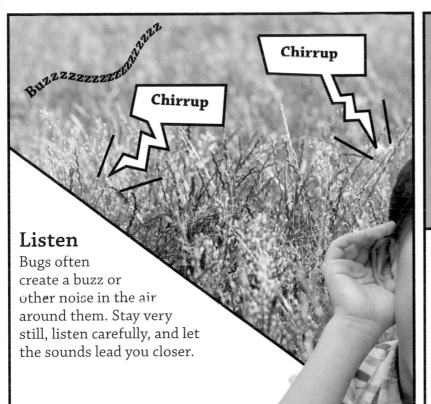

Listen

Bugs often create a buzz or other noise in the air around them. Stay very still, listen carefully, and let the sounds lead you closer.

Act fast

Quick reactions are essential on a bug hunt. Many bugs have sharp eyesight and super speed, so you must make your move without delay.

Take notes

Draw the bugs you find and describe them in detail. You can even turn your collection of notes and drawings into a brilliant bug book.

Let them go

When you have finished, release bugs near the spot where you found them. Place them on the ground gently to avoid hurting them.

A bug's home

Whether high in the treetops or deep underground, splashing in water or building a nest, bugs make themselves at home all over the world. Take this quiz to find out which bug lives where.

Tree
2

From its roots and trunk to its branches and leaves, a tree can provide safe shelter for many bugs.

Pond
1

Freshwater ponds and streams are full of life. Some bugs that live near these waters eat algae.

A

Ant
Thousands of ants live together in colonies. They build and maintain homes that are ruled by a queen.

B

Webspinner
These tropical insects have silk glands. They spin webs in leafy locations and eat moss, bark, and leaves.

C

Wasp
Among the busiest bugs, these high-fliers chew wood and use the pulp to build their homes.

3 Nest
These crafted homes are built in the trees using wooden fibres chewed by hard-working bugs.

Hive
A swarm of activity, hives are buzzing homes created using soft wax carried by flying bugs.

4

Underground
A huge colony of creatures creates an underground home with vast networks of tunnels and chambers.

5

Hidden trap
Watch your footing! Soil and leaves on the forest floor can be a secret covering for a hideaway burrow home beneath.

6

D Trapdoor spider
Secretive silk-spinning spiders make secure homes in dark places where they can trap food and lay eggs.

E Mayfly
This short-lived flying insect spends its time hunting for food, such as algae, and laying its eggs in water.

F Honeybee
Worker honeybees gather in their thousands to build complex homes high above the ground.

Defences

When it comes to avoiding being eaten, only the creatures with the best defences survive. Over time, bugs have developed some of the coolest defences in the entire animal kingdom.

Thorn bugs
Tiny treehoppers known as thorn bugs are masters of disguise. How many can you find in this photograph?

Defensive measures

Some bugs go to extremes to prevent or get away from enemy attack. From spikes and sprays to stinks and springs, these bugs show self-defence at its best.

Red-spotted purple butterfly

This butterfly looks beautifully bright to humans, but its colours appear poisonous to predators.

Click beetle

The click beetle uses its elytra to spring into the air, making a loud "click" sound as it escapes danger.

Camouflaged

With a body that closely resembles a plant thorn, this sneaky little insect is hidden in plain sight.

All together now

By grouping up, thorn bugs make a branch look like a spiky surface to confuse predators.

Bombardier beetle

Predators should beware the bombardier beetle, which sprays a toxic fluid when threatened.

Postman caterpillar

The postman caterpillar's big spikes make hungry predators think twice about attacking.

Stinkbug

Stinkbugs stand guard over their young. They also can release a nasty smell from their stomach.

Mosquito

The loud whining sound mosquitoes make comes from their wings flapping 400 times a second. Mosquitoes fly around at night looking for animals whose blood they can drink.

eeeeeeeeeeeeeeeeeeeeeeeeeeeeeeeeeeeee!

Deathwatch beetle

The deathwatch beetle taps its head on wood to attract a mate and to break down the wood for food. This insect got its name when people heard it tapping late at night as they sat up with sick loved ones.

tap tap tap tap tap tap tap tap tap tap tap

Buzzzzzzzzzzzzz

Wasp

The wings of a wasp make a buzzing sound while they fly. When their nests are being threatened, wasps flap their wings faster, creating an even louder buzz to scare away the enemy.

Noise-makers

Considering their small size, some bugs can make a very big noise! Many of them make sounds by rubbing parts of their bodies together. This makes noises from whining to chirruping, which they use to communicate, find a mate, or scare away attackers.

Giant cicada

The winner of the loudest bug award goes to the male giant cicada. Small drums on their bodies, called tymbals, make a high-pitched sound that can be heard 1.6 km (1 mile) away.

chirrup!

!

LOUDEST BUG!

Hissssssssssssssssssssssss!

Hissing cockroach

Madagascar's hissing cockroach sounds like a snake. The male pushes air out through breathing holes to make a loud hiss that scares away attackers and impresses females.

Sound engineer

The male mole cricket finds a mate using a song. He digs a burrow entrance shaped like a trumpet and sits at the bottom making a churring sound. The shape of the entrance means the sound can be heard from 2 km (1.2 miles) away.

Trumpet-shaped entrance to make the sound louder

Main burrow

Strong legs for burrowing

Rubs wings to make sound

Glow in the dark

Like a magical sea of lights shining in the dark, glowing insects are a spectacular sight. They can produce their own night light to attract mates or other insects to eat. This amazing feat is called bioluminescence, which means "biological light".

Fireflies
These beetles are nocturnal, which means they are active at night. Male fireflies glow yellow, orange, or green, or flash light patterns to attract females.

Great glowers

Fireflies aren't the only bugs that glow. Meet two other incredible insects that light up in unexpected ways.

Click beetle at night

Click beetle

Tropical species of click beetle glow from two green "headlight" spots, as well as a spot under their bodies. These lights get brighter if the beetle feels threatened.

Railroad worm with all its lights on

Railroad worm

Railroad worms are not really worms – they're actually beetle larvae. This nocturnal creature makes greenish-yellow lights along its body and a red light from its head. It can turn off its side lights when hunting for bugs to eat.

Extreme survivors

Bugs are some of the toughest creatures on Earth, and many of them thrive in extreme environments. From the sizzling heat to the freezing cold, and even in life-threatening conditions, these bugs continue to come out on top.

In the cold

As the temperature drops, most bugs hide out by trees and rocks and save their energy to keep warm. Only the most extreme bugs can survive the punishing cold without worry.

Water collector
In Africa's Namib Desert, the darkling beetle catches water droplets from ocean fog on its body before tipping them into its mouth.

Water droplets

In the heat

Animals in very hot environments usually look for shelter from strong sunlight or move only at night to keep cool. But these two extreme bugs don't mind spending a day out in the heat.

Sand survivor
During the hottest part of the day, Sahara Desert ants eat insects that have died in the scorching Sun.

In a disaster

People wouldn't last long in ice or boiling water, but some bugs are better survivors than humans. Meet the bugs that triumph in the face of danger.

Cool caterpillar

The Arctic woolly bear caterpillar can actually survive being frozen most of the time before thawing out when the weather gets warmer in summer.

Mountain mover

At home in the snowy mountains, the Himalayan jumping spider doesn't mind hunting for prey in the cold. It has strong legs and excellent eyesight.

Cannibal cockroaches

Cockroaches do well in emergency situations because they'll eat anything, including each other if necessary!

Toxic home

Tiny crustaceans like this yeti crab live in the pitch-black, superhot waters near deep ocean vents. They survive by eating toxic bacteria released by the vents.

Get to work

These insects are hard workers. The jobs they do in the natural world, from spreading pollen to taking care of pests, have big benefits for our daily lives. Some of the products they make are turned into useful fabrics and delicious foods.

! WOW!

A **worker bee** makes about **one-twelfth** of a teaspoon of **honey** in its lifetime.

The gardener

Bees transfer pollen between different flowers in a process called pollination.

The farmer

Some insects, such as ants, eat harmful pests like aphids, which could destroy crops.

Pollination keeps our gardens in bloom and helps 90 per cent of wild plants to flower.

With fewer pests to cause damage, our harvest grows bigger and stronger.

Bugs on the menu

In many cultures, humans eat bugs as food. Whether cooked or served raw, ants, beetles, crickets, locusts, and worms are common snacks in some countries. Bugs can also make food that people enjoy eating, like the sweet honey produced by bees.

Eating bugs

Honey

The cleaner

Dung beetles roll poo into a neat ball. They may bury the ball, or lay their eggs inside it.

Our environment and farmlands are cleaner, and the buried poo returns nutrients to the soil.

The tailor

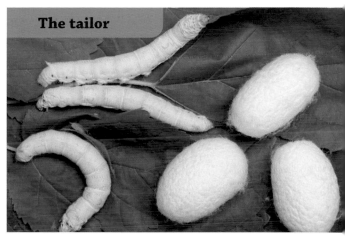

As caterpillars, silk worms spend days spinning protective silk cocoons.

We spin the cocoons into the fabric silk, which is used to make clothes and other goods.

Top bugs

With so many different types of bug in the world, there is plenty of competition to be the best. From the smallest bug to the longest bug, and from the fastest bug to the bug with the fastest bite, here is the winner in each category.

Biggest wingspan

The atlas moth from Asia is the world's largest moth. Its has a wingspan that can measure up to 25 cm (10 in) long.

Longest lifespan

The termite queen can live for up to 50 years. Worker termites have a much shorter lifespan at only 1–2 years.

Shortest lifespan

A mayfly rarely survives longer than a day. It only has time to mate and lay eggs before it dies. Some survive for only 30 minutes.

Strongest bug

The horned dung beetle can pull more than 1,100 times its own body weight. That's the same as a person lifting six double-decker buses!

Fastest bug

The tiger beetle is the speediest bug, reaching 9 kph (5 mph). This works out at 125 times its body length every second.

Fastest bite

The trap jaw ant can snap its jaws together at 233 kph (145 mph). That's 2,300 times faster than the blink of an eye.

Longest jump

The froghopper uses its strong muscles to leap up to 70 cm (27 in) into the air. That's up to 70 times its own height!

The millipede has more legs than any living creature. Some have more than 700 legs, but most have up to 400 legs.

Loudest bug

The giant cicada is the noisiest bug on Earth. Its call is louder than a motorbike and can be heard 1.6 km (1 mile) away.

Heaviest bug

The giant weta is the biggest bug ever discovered. It can weigh up to 71 g (2.5 oz), which is three times more than a mouse!

Fastest flying bug

Dragonflies are the fastest flying bugs in the world. When they fly, they can reach speeds of up to 50 kph (30 mph).

Smallest bug

The fairy fly can be one-quarter of the size of a full stop. These tiny wasps are everywhere but too small to be easily seen.

Longest bug

The stick insect can grow up to 56 cm (22 in) in length. Its long body helps the bug to hide among tree branches.

Bug facts and figures

Bugs are amazing creatures. Here are some weird and wonderful facts you might not know about them!

Periodical cicadas spend either **13 or 17 years** underground before all coming out at once.

10,000,000,000,

100

A cat flea can jump about 100 times its body length.

5,000

A ladybird can eat up to 5,000 insects in its lifetime.

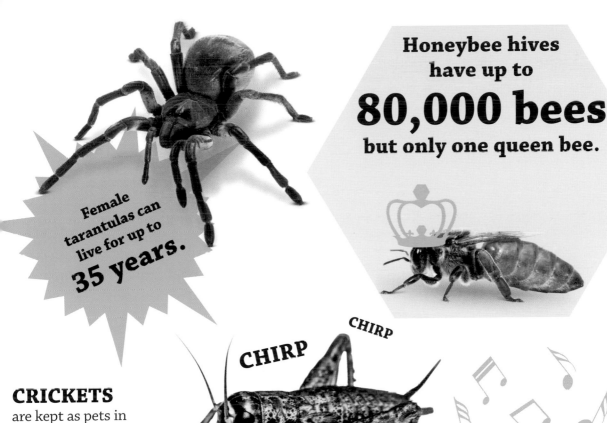

Female tarantulas can live for up to **35 years.**

Honeybee hives have up to **80,000 bees** but only one queen bee.

CHIRP

CHIRP

CRICKETS
are kept as pets in some countries because people like the sound of their chirp.

000,000,000

(10 quintillion) is the number of insects in the world.

1.5

Stink bugs are so smelly you can smell their toxic odour 1.5 m (5 ft) away.

6 m

(20 ft) is how high some species of termites build their mounds.

Glossary

Here are the meanings of some words that are useful for you to know when learning about bugs.

abdomen The rear section of an insect's body

adaptation Way in which an animal or plant becomes better-suited to its habitat

algae Simple plants found in or near water. Seaweeds are a type of algae

antennae Pair of sense organs, also called feelers, located near the front of an insect's head

arachnid Type of arthropod with eight legs and two body sections, such as a spider

arthropod Group of invertebrates with a tough outer skeleton, jointed legs, and segmented body

bioluminescence Chemical reaction in which an animal produces light

camouflage Colours or patterns on an animal's exterior that help it to blend in with the environment

chrysalis Hard casing a butterfly wraps itself in during metamorphosis

climate The weather that is usual for an area over a long period of time

colony Group of insects that live together

crops Group of plants that are grown as food

This katydid is camouflaged as a leaf.

crustacean Type of arthropod with a pair of two-part limbs on each body segment and two pairs of antennae. Lobsters, crabs, and shrimp are crustaceans

defence How an animal or plant protects itself from predators or the environment

elytra Hard outer wings of a beetle

entomologist Scientist who studies bugs

environment Place where an animal or plant lives

forewing Front wing of an animal

fossil Remains of a dead animal or plant that have been preserved in rock over time

habitat Natural home of an animal or plant

halteres Little club-like knobs on a true fly where another insect's hind wings would be

insect Type of arthropod with six legs and a three-part body

invertebrate Animal without a backbone

labella Spongy mouthparts on a true fly used to take in liquids

larvae Young of certain insects, such as a wasp

metamorphosis Process by which some animals transform themselves into a different form from youth to adulthood. For example, a caterpillar into a butterfly

myriapod Type of arthropod with many legs, such as a millipede

nectar Sweet liquid made by some flowers

nocturnal Animals that sleep during the day and are active at night

nutrients Types of food that animals and plants need to survive

nymph Young of certain insects, such as a locust

parasite Animal that lives on and feeds off the blood of another animal, harming its host in the process

pest Animal that attacks or destroys things, such as crops

pesticide Chemical that farmers use to control pests

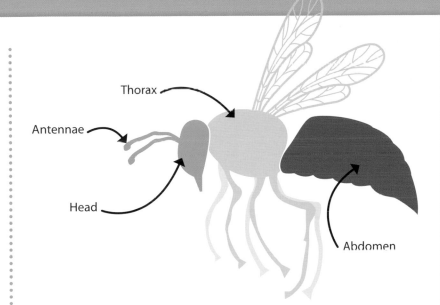

Thorax

Antennae

Head

Abdomen

poisonous Animal or plant that may be deadly if touched or eaten

pollen Powder that comes from flowering plants and aids in pollination

pollination Transfer of pollen from one plant to another by insects such as bees and butterflies

predator Bug or other animal that hunts other living animals for food

prey Bug or other animal that is hunted for food

proboscis Long, tube-shaped mouthpart some insects have to suck up liquids

rostrum Thin, beak-shaped mouthpart true bugs have to suck up liquids

scavenger Animal that feeds on the remains of another animal that has already died, whether by a predator attack or natural causes

species Specific types of animal or plant with shared features that can mate and produce young together

thorax Middle segment of an insect, between the abdomen and head

toxic Substance that is dangerous, such as poison

wingspan Length between the two tips of a pair of wings

vegetation Plant life found in a particular habitat

venom Harmful substance released by an animal or plant, by a sting or fangs

Index

Acknowledgements

The publisher would like to thank the following people for their assistance in the preparation of this book: Dan Crisp and Bettina Myklebust Stovne for illustrations; Fiona Macdonald and Ala Uddin for additional design; Jayati Sood for picture research; Caroline Hunt for proofreading; Hilary Bird for compiling the index; and Jessica Honaker and Kristie Reddick of The Bug Chicks for their "Meet the experts" interview.

The publisher would like to thank the following for their kind permission to reproduce their photographs:

(Key: a-above; b-below/bottom; c-centre; f-far; l-left; r-right; t-top)

(Key: a-above; b-below/bottom; c-centre; f-far; l-left; r-right; t-top)

1 **FLPA:** Piotr Naskrecki / Minden Pictures (c). **2 Alamy Stock Photo:** blickwinkel / Teigler (br). **3 123RF.com:** Nataliia Kravchuk (cr). **Alamy Stock Photo:** General Stock (crb); Andre Skonieczny (tc). **4-5 Science Photo Library:** Walter Myers (ca). **5 Dorling Kindersley:** Natural History Museum, London (cb). **Dreamstime.com:** Paul Fleet (tl); Willyambradberry (tr). **6 Alamy Stock Photo:** AlessandraRCstock (br). **Amazon-Images** (cr). **Dorling Kindersley:** Thomas Marent (cl). **6-7 Dorling Kindersley:** Ed Merritt. **7 Alamy Stock Photo:** Nigel Cattlin (ca); Photoshot (cl); Graphic Science (cb). **Getty Images:** Tim Graham (tr). **8 Dorling Kindersley:** Tyler Christensen (clb). **10 Alamy Stock Photo:** Mark Moffett / Minden Pictures (bc). **10-11 Alamy Stock Photo:** F. Rauschenbach (c). **11 Alamy Stock Photo:** Darlyne A. Murawski (br); Scenics & Science (bl). **Science Photo Library:** John Walsh (cra). **12-13 123RF.com:** Subrata Chakraborty / signout (ca). **Alamy Stock Photo:** Christian Musat (cb). **Getty Images:** Paul Starosta (b); Claudius Thiriet (t). **15 Alamy Stock Photo:** Minden Pictures (ca). **Dreamstime.com:** Janmiko1 (cl). 1**6 Alamy Stock Photo:** Jack Thomas (cb). **Dorling Kindersley:** Natural History Museum, London (c); Natural History Museum, London (bc). **17 Alamy Stock Photo:** Domiciano Pablo Romero Franco (clb, cr); Adam Gault (crb, cb). **Fotolia:** photomic (tl). **18 Dorling Kindersley:** Thomas Marent (cl). **19 123RF.com:** Ian Grainger (cla). **iStockphoto.com:** surajps (bl). **20 Dorling Kindersley:** Gyuri Csoka Cyorgy (cr); Jerry Young (tl); Jerry Young (br). **21 Alamy Stock Photo:** Barrett & MacKay (cb); Daniel Borzynski (c). **Getty Images:** Andia (ca). **22 123RF.com:** alekss (bc). **23 Alamy Stock Photo:** FLPA (crb). **Dreamstime.com:** Wollertz (clb). **Getty Images:** mikroman6 (tr). **24-25 123RF.com:** Nawin Nachiangmai (c). **25 Alamy Stock Photo:** blickwinkel / Hartl (br); Daniel Borzynski (cb). **26 123RF.com:** Zhang YuanGeng (cb). **Science Photo Library:** Eye Of Science (bc). **27 Alamy Stock Photo:** blickwinkel / Sturm (cb); Natural History Museum, London (ca). **Dreamstime.com:** Herman5551 (bc). **28 Alamy Stock Photo:** Brian Bevan (tc); Andre Skonieczny (cra). **28-29 Alamy Stock Photo:** General Stock (c).

30 Dorling Kindersley: Thomas Marent (cr); Natural History Museum, London (cb). **31 Alamy Stock Photo:** Andrew Darrington (cl). **Dorling Kindersley:** Natural History Museum, London (cra); Natural History Museum, London (c); Natural History Museum, London (cb). **32 Alamy Stock Photo:** Survivalphotos (c); Thomas Kitchin & Victoria Hurst (cb); Thomas Kitchin & Victoria Hurst (bc). **32-33 Alamy Stock Photo:** Thomas Kitchin & Victoria Hurst. **33 Alamy Stock Photo:** Survivalphotos (crb). **34 Alamy Stock Photo:** Mike Mckavett (cl); Premaphotos (crb). **35 123RF.com:** Morley Read (tc). **Alamy Stock Photo:** Chris Mattison (c). **FLPA:** Piotr Naskrecki / Minden Pictures (bc). **36 Alamy Stock Photo:** Lifes All White (clb); Lars S. Madsen (cb). **iStockphoto.com:** digitalr (crb). **37 Alamy Stock Photo:** David Chapman (cr); Nature Photographers Ltd (tl). **iStockphoto.com:** digitalr (bl). **38 123RF.com:** Nataliia Kravchuk (cl/1st Bug in Below circle, cl/4th bug in Below circle); Sirichai Raksue (clb); Nataliia Kravchuk (cl/2nd bug in Below circle, cl/3rd bug in Below circle). Alamy Stock Photo: Cristina Lichti (cla/Bugs in Above circle). **Dreamstime.com:** Isselee (fclb). **39 123RF.com:** Mariusz Jurgielewicz (crb). **40 courtesy of The Bug Chicks:** (tl). **41 courtesy of The Bug Chicks. 42 Getty Images:** Antagain (cr). **43 123RF.com:** Parinya Binsuk (ca); Damian Sromek (tl); Igor Terekhov (tr). **44 Alamy Stock Photo:** blickwinkel / Hecker (cb). **46-47 Alamy Stock Photo:** Martin Shields (t). **46 Alamy Stock Photo:** Zoonar GmbH (crb); Steven Russell Smith (cb). **47 Getty Images:** Moment Open (crb). **naturepl.com:** Nature Production (clb). **48 Alamy Stock Photo:** Wildlife Gmbh (cl). **FLPA:** G E Hyde (cr). **49 123RF.com:** Oleksandr Kostiuchenko (bl). **Alamy Stock Photo:** Sabena Jane Blackbird (cr). **Getty Images:** Science Photo Library (tl). **50 Alamy Stock Photo:** Phil Degginger (bc). **50-51 Alamy Stock Photo:** Floris van Breugel / naturepl. com. **51 Alamy Stock Photo:** Kim Taylor (cra). **Dreamstime.com:** Darius Baužys (ca). **Getty Images:** Robert F. Sisson (crb). **52 Alamy Stock Photo:** Michael & Patricia Fogden / Minden Pictures (cl, clb). **Getty Images:** Visuals Unlimited, Inc. / Louise Murray (cr). **naturepl.com:** Nick Upton (cb). **52-53 naturepl.com:** Gavin Maxwell (bc). **53 Alamy Stock Photo:** Maximilian Weinzierl (cr). **naturepl.com:** David Shale (crb). **54 Dorling Kindersley:** RHS Hampton Court Flower Show 2011 (clb). **Dreamstime.com:** Branex (crb); Natalia Miachikova (cr). **55 Alamy Stock Photo:** Horst Klemm (cl); Ton Koene (tc). **Dreamstime.com:** Gee807 (clb); Sofiaworld (cr). **56 Alamy Stock Photo:** Bazzano Photography (cb); Mitsuhiko Imamori / Minden Pictures (cl); blickwinkel / Teigler

(clb); blickwinkel (cr); Nick Upton (c). **Dorling Kindersley:** Claire Cordier (tr); Neil Fletcher (crb). **57 Alamy Stock Photo:** Sabena Jane Blackbird (cl); Mark Moffett / Minden Pictures (cra). **Getty Images:** Graeme Robertson (crb). **Science Photo Library:** Dr. Harold Rose (cb). **58 Dorling Kindersley:** Natural History Museum, London (cra). **Dreamstime.com:** Aaskolnick (cl). 59 **123RF.com:** Ameng Wu / amwu (tl); Wanlop Sonngam (c). **Dreamstime.com:** Meisterphotos (bl). **60 123RF. com:** Morley Read (bc). **Dreamstime.com:** Herman5551 (tl). **29 FLPA:** Image Broker (cla)**Front Endpapers: Dorling Kindersley:** Natural History Museum, London (ca), Natural History Museum, London 0cb; **Back Endpapers: Science Photo Library:** Louise Hughes 0ca

Cover images: Front: 123RF.com: Rueangsin Phuthawil cla, Apisit Wilaijit cra; **Dorling Kindersley:** Gyuri Csoka Cyorgy ca, Natural History Museum, London c; **FLPA:** Piotr Naskrecki / Minden Pictures cb; **Front Flap: 123RF.com:** Nawin Nachiangmai cl; **Alamy Stock Photo:** blickwinkel / Sturm c; **Dorling Kindersley:** Natural History Museum, London cla; **Dreamstime.com:** Meisterphotos cr; **Back Flap: Alamy Stock Photo:** Nature Photographers Ltd br; **iStockphoto.com:** digitalr cra

All other images © Dorling Kindersley
For further information see: www.dkimages.com

My Findout facts:

Why don't insects grow bigger?

You will never see an insect that's as big as an elephant! An insect that big would be crushed by the weight of its external skeleton, or exoskeleton. It also wouldn't be able to breathe: Instead of lungs, insects have tiny holes on their body called spiracles that slowly take in oxygen from the air. Bigger animals need lungs or gills to get enough oxygen to survive.

Spiracle up close

How are insects measured?

An insect's length is from the tip of its head to the end of its body. Antennae, legs, and wings aren't included. Each insect shown here is the longest that type of insect usually gets. But there are exceptions – like the longest stick insect ever measured, which was 56 cm (22 in)!

Froghopper
6 mm (¼ in)

Mantidfly
1.5 cm (⅝ in)

Mayfly
1 mm (0.03 in)

Silverfish
1 cm (½ in)

Bumble bee
2 cm (¾ in)

Periodical cicada
3 cm (1¼ in)

Madagascan hissing cockroach
6 cm (2⅜ in)